Giraffes
Up Close

Carmen Bredeson

E Enslow Elementary

CONTENTS

WORDS TO KNOW

adult (uh DULT)—Grown up.

grind (GRYND)—To crush into small pieces.

herds (HURDZ)—Groups of animals that live together.

tuft (TUFT)—A bunch of hair held together at one end.

Parts of a Giraffe

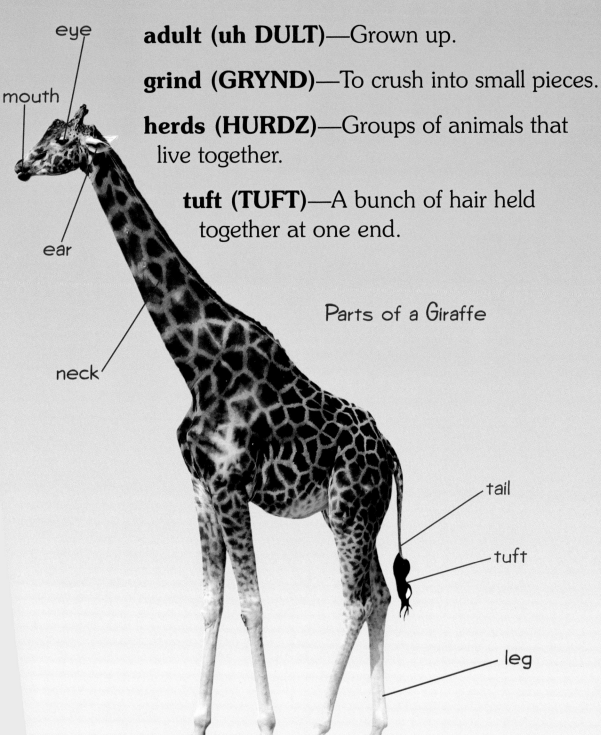

eye

mouth

ear

neck

tail

tuft

leg

GIRAFFE HOMES

Giraffes are the tallest animals in the world. They live in dry, grassy parts of Africa. Mothers and their babies live in **herds**. Most giraffes stay in the area of Africa where they were born.

Giraffes live in these shaded parts of Africa.

GIRAFFE FUR

UP CLOSE

A giraffe's fur is covered with spots. Each giraffe has different spots. The spots help giraffes hide among the trees. Lions are the only animals that will attack an **adult** giraffe.

GIRAFFE TONGUE

UP CLOSE

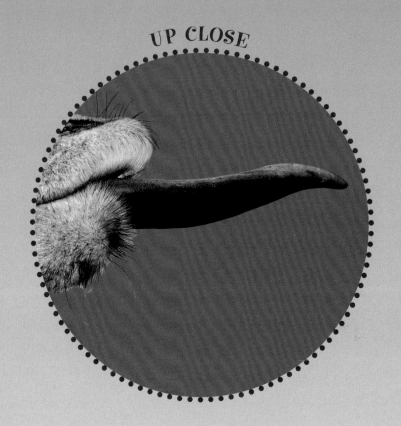

Giraffes eat leaves from the tops of trees.
Only elephants can reach as high as giraffes.
The giraffe lifts its head. It sticks out its long
black tongue. The tongue wraps around
a branch.

GIRAFFE TEETH
UP CLOSE

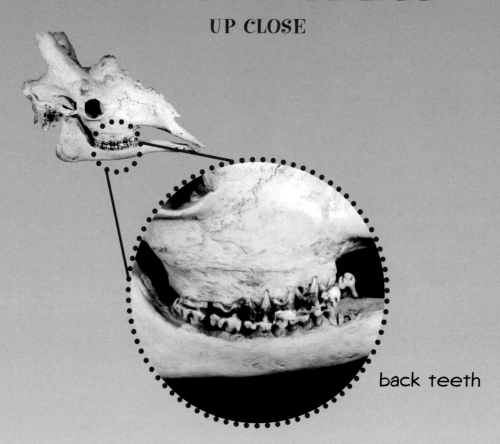

back teeth

The giraffe pulls the branch into its mouth.
Its back teeth **grind** up the leaves. A giraffe
can eat 75 pounds of leaves a day!

GIRAFFE NECK

A giraffe's neck is very long. It has seven neck bones, just like people. Giraffe neck bones are much longer than ours. A giraffe usually sleeps standing up. Sometimes it rests its neck on a tree branch.

GIRAFFE EYES

UP CLOSE

Giraffes can see from high up. They can spot a lion before it gets too close. When a giraffe sees a lion, it spreads its ears and flicks its tail. This warns the rest of the herd of danger. The herd gets ready to run.

GIRAFFE TAIL

UP CLOSE

A giraffe's tail is VERY long. Some giraffe tails reach almost to the ground. There is a **tuft** of black hair at the end of the tail. The giraffe moves its tail back and forth to chase away bugs.

GIRAFFE LEGS

UP CLOSE

A giraffe's leg is as tall as a man. To walk, a
giraffe moves both legs on one side of its body.
Then it moves both legs on the other side.
Giraffes can run very fast for a short time.

GIRAFFE BABY

UP CLOSE

Giraffes give birth standing up. The baby giraffe falls to the ground. It can walk soon after it is born. That helps it escape from enemies like crocodiles, leopards, and lions.

LIFE CYCLE

BABY—Can weigh 150 pounds at birth.

YOUNG—Are full grown by age 5.

ADULT—Can live to be 25 years old.

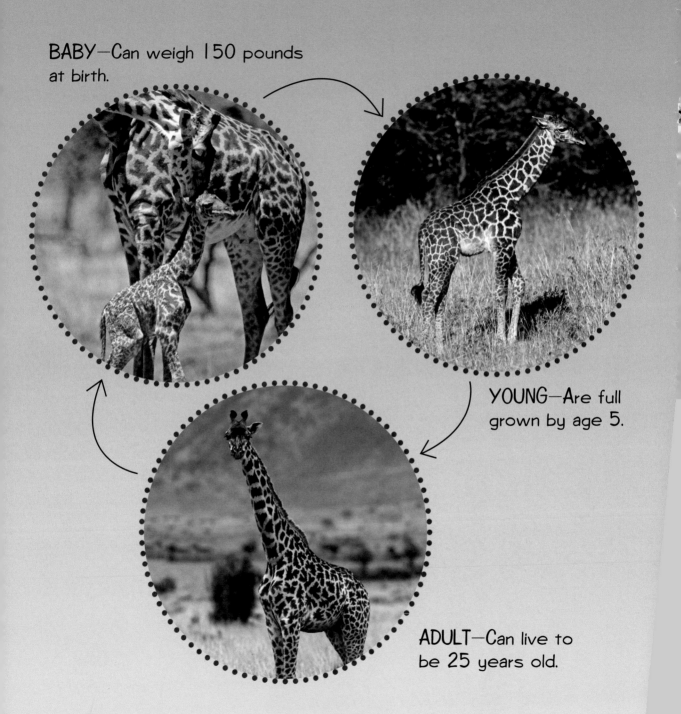

LEARN MORE

BOOKS

In English

Tourville, Amanda Doering. *A Giraffe Grows Up*. Minneapolis, Minn.: Picture Window Books, 2007.

Parker, Barbara. *Giraffes*. Minneapolis, Minn.: Carolrhoda Books, 2004.

In English and Spanish / En inglés y español

Macken, JoAnn Early. *Giraffes / Las jirafas*. Milwaukee, Wis.: Weekly Reader Early Learning Library, 2003.

WEB SITES

Enchanted Learning
<www.enchantedlearning.com/themes/giraffe.shtml>

National Geographic Kids
<www.nationalgeographic.com/kids/creature_feature/0111/giraffes.html>

INDEX

Series Literacy Consultant:
Allan A. De Fina, Ph.D.
Past President of the New Jersey Reading Association
Chairperson, Department of Literacy Education
New Jersey City University
Jersey City, New Jersey

Science Consultant:
Patrick Thomas, Ph.D.
General Curator
Bronx Zoo
Wildlife Conservation Society
Bronx, New York

Note to Parents and Teachers: The **Zoom In on Animals!** series supports the National Science Education Standards for K–4 science. The Words to Know section introduces subject-specific vocabulary words, including pronunciation and definitions. Early readers may need help with these new words.

Enslow Elementary, an imprint of Enslow Publishers, Inc.
Enslow Elementary® is a registered trademark of Enslow Publishers, Inc.

Copyright © 2009 by Carmen Bredeson

Library of Congress Cataloging-in-Publication Data

Bredeson, Carmen.
Giraffes up close / Carmen Bredeson.
p. cm. — (Zoom in on animals!)
Summary: "Provides an up-close look at giraffes for new readers"—Provided by publisher.
Includes bibliographical references and index.
ISBN-13: 978-0-7660-3081-7
ISBN-10: 0-7660-3081-4
1. Giraffe—Juvenile literature. I. Title.
QL737.U56B74 2008
599.638—dc22   2007034800

Printed in the United States of America

10 9 8 7 6 5 4 3 2 1

To Our Readers: We have done our best to make sure all Internet Addresses in this book were active and appropriate when we went to press. However, the author and the publisher have no control over and assume no liability for the material available on those Internet sites or on other Web sites they may link to. Any comments or suggestions can be sent by e-mail to comments@enslow.com or to the address on the back cover.

♻ Enslow Publishers, Inc., is committed to printing our books on recycled paper. The paper in every book contains 10% to 30% post-consumer waste (PCW). The cover board on the outside of each book contains 100% PCW. Our goal is to do our part to help young people and the environment too!

Photo Credits: © Arthur Morris/Visuals Unlimited, p. 12; © 1999, Artville, LLC, p. 5 (map); © Barbara Gerlach/Visuals Unlimited, p. 22 (top right, bottom); © Carol Walker/naturepl.com, p. 21; Courtesy of Altaileopard, p. 5 (map shading); © Horst Klemm/Masterfile, p. 19; © iStockphoto.com/Frank Parker, p. 20; © iStockphoto.com/Thomas Voss, p. 16; © Jean Michel Labat/ardea.com, p. 9; Jeff Foott/Discovery Channel Images/Getty Images, p. 17; © Joe McDonald/Visuals Unlimited, p. 22 (top left); © 2007 Jupiterimages Corporation, pp. 4–5, 6, 13, 15, 18; © Ken Lucas/Visuals Unlimited, p. 10; © Nicholas Pitt/Alamy, p. 7; Peter Firus/Flagstaffotos, p. 14; © Richard Du Toit/naturepl.com, p. 11; © Scientifica/Visuals Unlimited, p. 8; Shutterstock, pp. 1, 3.

Front Cover Photos: © 2007 Jupiterimages Corporation (center right); Peter Firus/Flagstaffotos (top right); © Scientifica/Visuals Unlimited (bottom right); Shutterstock (left).

Back Cover Photo: © Richard Du Toit/naturepl.com

Enslow Elementary
an imprint of
Enslow Publishers, Inc.
40 Industrial Road
Box 398
Berkeley Heights, NJ 07922
USA
http://www.enslow.com